HAL•LEONARD INSTRUMENTAL PLAY-ALONG

AUDIO ACCESS INCLUDED

SOLO ARRANGEMENTS OF
12 FAVORITES WITH
AUDIO ACCOMPANIMENT

OBOE

Disney Greats

T0052782

To access audio visit:
www.halleonard.com/mylibrary

Enter Code
2029-3476-1876-9116

ISBN 978-0-634-09683-9

Walt Disney Music Company
Wonderland Music Company, Inc.

DISTRIBUTED BY

HAL•LEONARD® CORPORATION

7777 W. BLUEMOUND RD. P.O. BOX 13819 MILWAUKEE, WI 53213

Visit Hal Leonard Online at
www.halleonard.com

Disney Greats

ARABIAN NIGHTS

from Walt Disney's ALADDIN

OBOE

Lyrics by HOWARD ASHMAN
Music by ALAN MENKEN

THE BARE NECESSITIES

from Walt Disney's THE JUNGLE BOOK

OBOE

Words and Music by
TERRY GILKYSON

A CHANGE IN ME

from Walt Disney's BEAUTY AND THE BEAST: THE BROADWAY MUSICAL

OBOE

Words by TIM RICE
Music by ALAN MENKEN

HAWAIIAN ROLLER COASTER RIDE

from Walt Disney's LILO & STITCH

OBOE

Words and Music by ALAN SILVESTRI
and MARK KEALI'I HO'OMALU

HONOR TO US ALL

from Walt Disney Pictures' MULAN

OBOE

Music by MATTHEW WILDER
Lyrics by DAVID ZIPPEL

9

legato

lightly

Small notes optional

I'M STILL HERE
(Jim's Theme)
from Walt Disney's TREASURE PLANET

OBOE

Words and Music by
JOHN RZEZNIK

11

IT'S A SMALL WORLD

from "IT'S A SMALL WORLD" at Disneyland Park and Magic Kingdom Park

OBOE

Words and Music by RICHARD M. SHERMAN
and ROBERT B. SHERMAN

THE MEDALLION CALLS

from Walt Disney Pictures' PIRATES OF THE CARIBBEAN: THE CURSE OF THE BLACK PEARL

OBOE

Music by KLAUS BADELT

LOOK THROUGH MY EYES

from Walt Disney Pictures' BROTHER BEAR

OBOE

Words and Music by
PHIL COLLINS

PROMISE

from MILLENNIUM CELEBRATION at Epcot

OBOE

Music by GAVIN GREENAWAY
Words by DON DORSEY

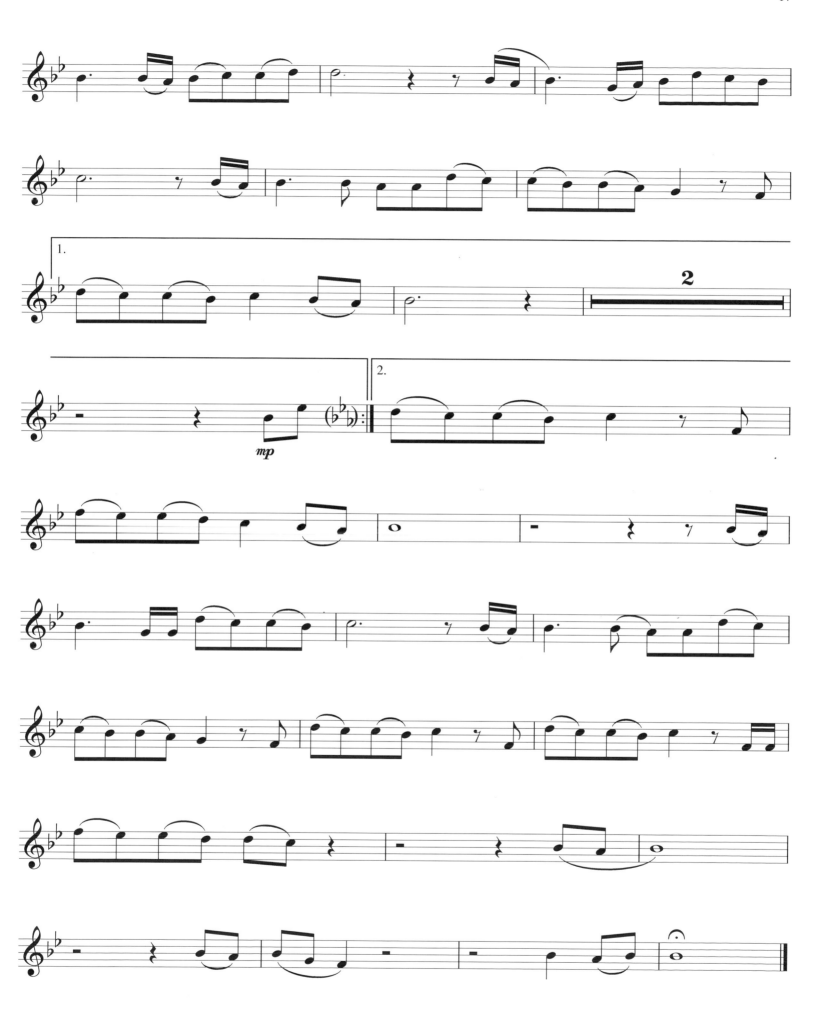

THE SIAMESE CAT SONG
from Walt Disney's LADY AND THE TRAMP

OBOE

Words and Music by PEGGY LEE
and SONNY BURKE

SUPERCALIFRAGILISTICEXPIALIDOCIOUS

from Walt Disney's MARY POPPINS

OBOE

Words and Music by RICHARD M. SHERMAN
and ROBERT B. SHERMAN

TWO WORLDS

from Walt Disney Pictures' TARZAN ™

OBOE

Words and Music by
PHIL COLLINS

WHERE THE DREAM TAKES YOU

from Walt Disney Pictures' ATLANTIS: THE LOST EMPIRE

OBOE

Lyrics by DIANE WARREN
Music by DIANE WARREN and JAMES NEWTON HOWARD

YO HO
(A Pirate's Life for Me)
from PIRATES OF THE CARIBBEAN at Disneyland Park and Magic Kingdom Park

OBOE

Words by XAVIER ATENCIO
Music by GEORGE BRUNS